# TEACHER TRICKS
## Second Edition
### BY

## DOUGLAS L. SIMMONS

WILLIAN

D0165364

Copyright ©1991 by Douglas L. Simmons
Published by Brite-Idea Publishing Company
1909 Sunset Drive
Walla Walla, Washington 99362

ISBN: 0-9627728-2-8

# PREFACE

Many teachers have long debated whether teaching is an art or science, and also, whether good teaching can really be taught or shared with new teachers. Basically, I feel that teaching is an art, but some things can be taught.

With this question in mind, I decided to prepare a handbook that would very simply list some of the tricks, and ideas that I have learned to use as a teacher. This handbook is not designed to be a guide for becoming a good teacher, but it is my hope that a future teacher, a new teacher, or a current teacher may be able to pick up one or two tricks or ideas that may be helpful to them in the classroom. If this is accomplished, then I feel that this handbook has accomplished its purpose.

LB
1025.3
.S5

# TABLE OF CONTENTS

Preface ............................................... 2

    I. Starting The School Year ........................... 5

   II. First Day of School ............................... 6

  III. Files ............................................. 6

  IV. Two Important People ............................. 6

    V. Grading Homework ............................... 7

  VI. Back-To-School Night ............................ 8

 VII. Conferences ...................................... 9

VIII. Discipline ........................................ 9

  IX. Insuring Learning ................................ 11

   X. Recommendations ................................ 13

  XI. Counselor ....................................... 14

 XII. First Teaching Job ................................ 14

XIII. Duplicating ....................................... 15

XIV. Being A Good Employee ........................... 16

 XV. Testing .......................................... 17

XVI. Grading .......................................... 22

XVII. A Final Word ...................................... 24

Appendix .............................................. 25

*To my parents*

*Eldon and Abbie Simmons*

# I. Starting The School Year

A. Buy your extra supplies.

In August, pens, pencils, paper, etc. are on sale. I buy pencils for my kids, because undoubtedly a certain number of students will forget their pencils. By providing pencils from time to time, you can minimize trips out of the classroom.

B. Look through your books and select your homework problems.

Make sure when you mark your homework problems that you try to use one color ink for each year. i.e. First year, I use blue; second year, I use red, etc. This way you do not use the same homework problems each year and it keeps your students honest and they will not save their homework papers from year to year in order to pass them on to other students.

C. Try to make up a syllabus for the first semester. (See Sample A)

The syllabus is designed more for the teacher than the student. It helps you keep yourself on schedule, especially if you included dates. It is also handy to hand out at different times of the year, so that you can better explain what your course is covering during the semester. For example, I like to hand it out at parents' nights and conferences.

D. Draw up grade sheet. (See Sample B)

You should try to type up a simple grade sheet on how you are going to grade your students. (See *Grading*)

E. Expectations (See Sample C)

This sheet should list your major expectations of the students. By clearly stating your expectations, it will be easier for your students to perform in the manner that you desire and helps in matters of discipline.

F. Rules and Regulations (See Sample D)

This sheet outlines your rules for the class. Be specific, and fair. Let your students know what your guidelines are. You are responsible for their behavior.

G. Posting

1. Hang up a copy of each of the above sheets and a time schedule in your classroom. This way they will be available for quick reference.
2. Post your fire exit directions.

H. Multiple copies

Try to run off enough copies of your syllabus, grade sheet, expectations, rules and regulations, so that they will be available for back-to-school nights and conferences.

I. Pick up your keys, grade book, class lists, and schedules.

J. Make sure you have a supply of attendance slips, chalk, note pads, staples, tape, etc.

K. Clear out your mail box.

## II. FIRST DAY OF THE YEAR

A. Set the tone for the year. It is very important for you and your students that they understand what is going to happen in your classes. This saves a lot of frustrations, discipline problems, grade problems, and conference problems, which translates into a lot of saved time and effort. Set a firm tone, be businesslike.

B. Hand out and discuss the following:
1. Course Syllabus
2. Grade Sheet
3. Expectations
4. Rules and Regulations

## III. FILES

A. Make sure you keep updated files which include copies of the following:
1. Tests (Keep by Chapters)
2. Worksheets (Keep by Chapters)
3. Quizzes (Keep by Chapters)
4. Objectives (Keep by Chapters)
5. Goals (Keep by Chapters)
6. Recommendations
7. Letters
   a. You may want your English teacher to check your writing.
   b. Have your principal read and OK any letter before you send it out.
8. Notes on individual parent conferences

B. Beg, borrow, or request a filing cabinet as soon as possible. Most classrooms have drawers that may be used for files.

C. Keep files locked.

D. Ask secretaries for a few manila folders, get more later.

E. It is always handy to have plenty of extra copies of your tests, worksheets, quizzes, objectives, goals, etc.

## IV. TWO IMPORTANT PEOPLE

A. It can be very helpful if the secretary and the custodian like you.
1. Try to say, "Good Morning" and "Good Afternoon."
2. They are full of information and they can keep you out of trouble and save you a lot of time.

3. Let the secretary know when you leave and return to school.
4. Remember, a good secretary almost runs a school.

# V. Grading Homework

A. Keep it simple.
    1. I use a +, ✔, −, or 0. (See *Grading System*)
        a. "+" means good job. (10 points on the computer)
        b. "✔" means OK, about average. (9 points)
        c. "−" means not so good. (8 points)
        d. "0" means didn't turn it in.(5 points)
    2. A lot of my collegues use a number system, for example; "8/12," which means a student received 8 right out of 12, but I find this too complex and students may not understand your interpretation of their work.

B. You don't have to grade it all.
    1. Sometimes I will collect an assignment, and not grade it. (Bad habit to get into.)
    2. Sometimes you can grade just an important part of the assignment.
    3. Do not collect the assignment, go over it in class.

C. A lot of teachers have students exchange papers. (I do not use this method, because I feel I want to know why and where a student is having success on his or her assignments. I also believe some students try to be a little too generous in grading their friend's assignments. You should have the grader sign the paper.)

D. Grade papers together. In math and science, I try to grade two or three papers at a time. I lay one paper on top of another. With the answer columns side by side. This saves a lot of time.

E. If possible try to grade papers while students are studying or doing their next assignment, but always keep yourself available to answer questions and give extra help. This can save a lot of night work.

F. Watch the length of assignments. They should be of reasonable length.

G. An answer column on the right side of the student's paper can be helpful in locating a student's answers.

H. Have students circle their answers.

I. Add some positive, good comments when possible.

J. Make a circle on paper when an answer is left out. This way you and the student will know that an answer was missing. This may prevent a student from complaining later that he did have an answer there.

K.  Mark spelling mistakes with SP. This helps make students better spellers and your English teachers friends for life.

L.  Grade papers as soon as possible.
    1.  I have always found it very difficult grading old papers because it seems like you should be done with the material.
    2.  There is more positive reinforcement when you can hand back papers sooner.

M.  Have the students turn their papers in at the beginning of the class. This is a handy rule to make at the beginning of the year, because it saves time and hassles, and it puts the responsibility on the students to turn them in.

N.  Have student hand back papers while class is getting settled. (I do not use this method because I do not like students to see each other's grades, but many teachers do.)

O.  Red marking pens (Flairs) make great grading tools.

P.  I put my papers to grade or to hand back in my teacher's book, that way I have them when I go to class or my office. Some teachers use a separate folder for each class.

# VI. BACK-TO-SCHOOL NIGHT

A.  Be happy and friendly!

B.  Be positive and forceful.

C.  Hand out your grade sheet.

D.  Hand out your syllabus or goals sheet.

E.  I love to ask for questions, but this is probably not a good idea for a new teacher.

F.  This is not the time to discuss a student's status with a parent. Have the parent come in for a conference.

G.  Avoid giving back a group of bad papers or a test on this day. During my first year of teaching, I handed back a bunch of tests with bad scores in a chemistry class on the morning of Back-To-School Night. That night the parents turned out in force and asked some very difficult questions.

H.  Make sure you introduce yourself.

I.  This is a good time to explain how much work you expect your students to do.

J.  Parents like demonstrations. For example, sometimes I will do a quick experiment in chemistry.

# VII. Conferences

A. Tell the parent or guardian that you like their child. Most parents seem to be subconsciously convinced that the reason their child is not doing well is because the teacher does not like their child. You should try to break this barrier.

B. Remember, logic becomes somewhat of a stranger when you are talking to a parent about their child. They love their child who is very precious to them.

C. Be reassuring and positive.

D. Stick with the facts.
   1. Show them test scores, quiz scores, and homework scores.
   2. Use concrete examples of actual behavior.

E. Encourage the parents to have their child come in for extra help.

# VIII. Discipline

A. Set out your rules on day one.
   1. Hand out copies of your rules and regulations. (See Sample D)
   2. Stick to these rules.

B. Be consistent.

C. The old saying "Don't smile till Christmas" has some merit to it especially for new teachers. You can always lighten up later.

D. Try not to interrupt the students when they are settled down and working. Some students see an interruption as a time to stop working and start visiting or causing problems.

E. Stopping problems.
   1. Stop and look at the offender. A stern look works well.
   2. Stop and speak directly to the offender.
      a. What are you doing?
      b. What should you be doing?
   3. Stop and pick up grade book and start making notations.
   4. Ask student to come in after class. It is best not to take on a student when he or she is with their friends or classmates. Students do not want to lose face.
   5. Move the offending student. Put the student in the back of the room or way up front.
   6. Establish a seating chart. Students may not like this, but it can be an effective way of handling problems.
   7. Have student report after school. You might require them to scrub desks or wash the walls or clean the floor or wash windows. Do not give extra homework or make

them study as punishment. Make sure they understand what they did wrong. *YOU SHOULD NEVER, NEVER BE IN A CLASSROOM ALONE WITH A STUDENT, WITH THE DOOR CLOSED!* A student could accuse you of anything and cause serious legal problems.

F. Remember, in a quiet class, at least some learning is taking place.

G. Keep your students busy. If you do not keep them busy, they will keep you busy.

H. Save yelling for special occasions. If you continually raise your voice, you just add to the noise level. (I once heard a teacher yell "shut up" or "be quiet" 20 times in 15 minutes with no results.)

I. Try to promote mutual respect between you and your students.
   1. I believe, for the student to respect the teacher, the teacher must respect the student.
   2. If the students respect you, they are not likely to cause you problems.

J. An inexperienced teacher should joke or kid with the students in a most judicious manner.
   1. It is only a very good teacher that can control this atmosphere and not let the kids run away with the joking.
   2. Most students like an unstructured, relaxed environment, but this is treacherous ground for an inexperienced teacher.

K. Be square with your students.
   1. Grade them fairly.
   2. Be on time.
   3. Get their papers back to them promptly.
   4. Do not belittle students or other staff members.
   5. Treat them with respect.
   6. Let them know that you care about them.

L. Use plenty of rewards.
   1. Try some of these comments on students' papers or in response during class discussions.
      a. Great!
      b. OK.
      c. Good job.
      d. That is close.
      e. Can someone help him with the answer?
      f. Good!
      g. All right.
      h. Better!
      i. You are great.
      j. Marvelous.

2. You have been a good class this week; no homework this weekend

M. Know your students' names. If a student is causing problems it helps to call them by their name.

N. Have every student bring a library book to class. If they finish early, they can read their book. This can be very effective at the Jr.-Hi level.

O. Kicking a student out of class is a last resort. (Know where to send them.)

P. Some students may be a problem because of their home life.
    1. Visit with the counselor frequently in order to stay informed and inform counselor about students who are having problems.
    2. You may want to send a student to the counselor if they are continual discipline problems. Make sure you know what your counselor will do with the student.

Q. Never strike or swear at a student.

## IX. INSURING LEARNING

A. Use memorization.
    1. If you really want your students to learn something for a long period of time, use memorization.
    2. It promotes good retention.
    3. Sets brain patterns that last for years and years.

B. Review
    1. Repetition insures deeper learning.
    2. Important information should be reviewed during the year.
    3. Start the class period with a quick review of what you did the last time in class.

C. Ask for questions.
    1. A clear understanding of what is going on in your classroom seems to help students learn.
    2. Compliment the student for asking a good question.
    3. Questions help review and clarify information.
    4. Questions help every level of student.
    5. Questions can help keep a class fresh and alive.

D. Use visual displays. Hearing and seeing improves retention more than using either separately.
    1. Use blackboard. Colored chalk may aid or clarify your presentation.
    2. Use charts.
    3. Give demonstrations.
        a. Students of all ages love these.

b. Use students to help out.
　4. Overhead projector can be helpful.
　　　a. It is good for large classes and projecting small objects.
　　　b. You face your students.
　　　c. If you have a media center, they sometimes have visual masters. These can be used to make transparencies.

E. Keep it simple.
　1. Make sure your students know the key, important points. Tell them precisely which are the important points.
　2. Make sure students know the words that you are using.
　　　a. Many times teachers use words or terminology that students do not use or understand.
　　　b. Require your students to memorize spellings and definitions of important terms.
　　　c. Explain terms, in a manner in which all students can understand.

F. Be organized.
　1. Have a syllabus. (See Sample A)
　2. Use your text for an organizational and scheduling guide.
　　　a. Hi-light important facts.
　　　b. Circle homework question and problems in your book, ahead of time.
　　　c. Make notes or comments in the margins about special or crucial points.
　　　d. Date your book, where you leave off at the end of each day.
　　　　　1. This helps you keep track of where you were in your book each day.
　　　　　2. This helps you plan for the following year. You can go back and see where you were last year.
　　　　　3. It helps you keep on schedule.
　3. Keep a journal, diary, or lesson plan book.
　　　a. This helps you evaluate your program.
　　　b. This helps track your progress.
　　　c. This is a good place to list things that worked well, or poorly for you.
　　　d. This really helps your planning for the next year.
　4. Lesson Plans
　　　a. For most teachers these can be very helpful.
　　　　　1. Warning! These can be very time consuming.
　　　　　2. Keep them simple.
　　　b. Most teachers use a lesson plan book.

    c. Be careful, rigidly adhering to a plan once it is written can sometimes lead to an inflexible teaching style. I always remember the time that I had a perfectly prepared class. I knew just what I wanted to cover. A boy raised his hand and I knew I had to stop and review what we had been doing the past few days. There went my perfect plan.

    d. Lesson plans can improve most peoples' teaching. Most experienced and good teachers do this more as a mental process than as a written process.

    e. Make sure you date your plans.

    f. Make notes on what worked and what did not.

G. Use enthusiasm and energy.
  1. Be excited about your subject.
    a. Raise your voice.
    b. Wave your hands.
    c. Move around.
    d. Use body language.
    e. Remember you are competing with T.V.
  2. Keeps the kids awake and more involved.
  3. Remember, you were not hired to entertain, but to teach. Used in moderation this type of instruction makes teaching and learning more interesting.

H. Give examples of how what you are teaching applies to the students' lives or society in general. For example, sulfuric acid is used in most car batteries.

I. Use numerous tests and quizzes.
  1. Students seem to study more when they know they are going to have a test or quiz.
  2. Going over your tests and quizzes also helps.
  3. Give students three or four questions or concepts to prepare for the next class period, then quiz over one of them.

## X. STUDENT AND TEACHER RECOMMENDATIONS

A. Keep a copy of every recommendation that you write.
  1. I put them in a manila folder.
  2. Sometimes a college will lose your copy and want a second copy.
  3. This is helpful when you need a guide for another recommendation, for another student, or college.

B. Use a word processor, if possible.
  1. It is very easy to store your recommendations on a disk.
  2. This method of storage will prove most helpful for writing multiple recommendations.

C. Be truthful, positive, and short.

D. When a student requests a recommendation, make sure you have that student remind you every so often of the deadline for the completion of the recommendation. It is very easy to put these away and forget about them.

E. Use your previous recommendations as a guide.
   1. This saves a lot of time.
   2. Starting from scratch makes writing a recommendation a chore.

F. Typed recommendations look more professional.

G. Students should furnish a self-addressed and stamped envelope.

## XI. COUNSELOR

A. Know your counselor!!!
   1. Never send a student to a counselor unless you have a good idea of how the counselor is going to help the student.
   2. The more you know, the better you can judge when, where, and why you should send a student to a counselor.

B. Talk to the counselor about student's problems before they become major conflicts. This can prevent future problems.

C. Report all signs of sexual or physical abuse to your counselor and principal, immediately. In our state, we are required by law to make such reports.

D. If you are having a problem with a student learning, ask the counselor to see their permanent record file and test scores. These can give you insight into the student's learning ability, especially if they are an over-achiever or an under-achiever.
   1. Be careful! Test scores do not tell the whole story.
      a. They tend to overlook very creative people.
      b. Over-achievers sometimes do poorly.
      c. Watch out for test's validity.

E. If you have a good counselor, he or she will prove to be a very good source of information and help.

## XII. FIRST TEACHING JOB

A. Locate the following as soon as possible.
   1. Faculty restroom.
   2. Your teaching rooms.
   3. Teacher manuals.
   4. Curriculum guide.
   5. Mailbox
   6. Keys
      a. Guard these with your life.

b. Principals get very upset when you lose these!

c. A master key is the key which carries largest responsibility because it gives access to all rooms in a school.

d. Every lock takes a certain pressure or twist or force to open it. Play with them.

7. Faculty room.

   a. If the teachers eat in this room, make sure you don't take somebody else's seat. Some teachers in our school have a special place they like to sit every day at lunch.

   b. If you drink coffee, chip in for the coffee and don't forget to bring your own cup.

   c. If you smoke, check to see if you can smoke in the faculty room.

   d. This is not a good place to visit about a student's problems.

   e. This is not a very good place to do your work because there are too many interruptions.

8. Duplicating machine or copying machine.

   a. Ask one of the secretaries about what the policies are on using the copy machines.

   b. Make sure you ask for a few spirit masters.

9. School calendar is a must for your planning.

10. Audio-visual equipment.

11. Faculty Handbook can provide a wealth of information, if the school has one.

B. Learn your colleagues names as soon as possible. You might begin with the ones in your teaching field or those who teach in rooms next door.

C. It is usually best to kind of keep quiet until you find out how things run and work in your school. Nobody likes a fresh teacher who knows it all.

D. Be punctual, firm, and well organized.

E. Ask the secretary how to use the phone and where to find your messages.

F. At your first faculty meeting, you will receive most of the information you will need about the beginning of school, i.e. calendars, schedules, room assignments, parking places, faculty lists, etc.

## XIII. DUPLICATING

A. Run plenty of copies. If I need 20 worksheets, I will run 60 of them. This way I can file the extras for future use. Next year they could be used or maybe the following year. They are always available if needed.

B. Type quizzes, tests, worksheets, etc. on plain white paper.
   1. You can use these masters to make copies on most copy machines.
   2. Typing makes for more professional copies and students appreciate this.
   3. I store my masters in the back of each file that contains the copies. If you need more copies, the master is right there.

C. If you get in a pinch, your secretary may be able to run your copies for you. If she isn't able to help out, remember she has her own duties which demand her time and attention.

D. Try to be careful where you discard ruined copies of your tests. Students may pick these up!

E. I use different colors of paper for different forms of the same test.

F. Using both sides of a sheet can save paper.

## XIV. Being A Good Employee

A. Don't make complaints your main topic of your conversation. This can only cause you more problems in the long run. Be positive and supportive.
   1. Do not give a student's grades to another student or parent.
   2. Do not complain about a student in the faculty room.
   3. Do not relate what a colleague has told you to anybody but another colleague. Be very careful what you tell to students and parents.
   4. If you have trouble with your boss, set up an appointment and talk with him/her.
      a. Do not complain to everybody else about your employer.

B. Be responsible.
   1. Be on time. Do not show up late for work or meetings. By arriving late you are telling people that your time is more important than their time.
   2. Be prepared and think ahead.
   3. Turn in the papers, forms, or information that your boss needs as soon as possible.
   4. Get your progress reports and grades in on time. Remember, that other people are waiting and depending on you.
   5. Make sure you do your lunchroom, hall, and recess duties without being reminded.

6. Stay within your budget. If you need more money, go ask.
7. Watch your language. You are a professional.

C. Make sure you try to greet people in the morning.

D. Be dedicated.
   1. Don't be the first person out of the door everyday after school.
   2. Attend some games, performances, or concerts.

E. Be loyal.

F. Be honest.
   1. Do not borrow anything without asking the principal.
   2. Do not borrow from other teachers without asking.

G. Do not be afraid to take the extra step.

H. Use lots of thank you notes. Everybody likes to be thanked.

I. Communicate clearly and carefully.

J. Be a team player. Try to do what is best for the students and the school.

# XV. TESTING

A. Tests should test for the information that you expect the student to know.

B. A test should be made up before you cover the information in class.
   1. By knowing exactly what you are testing for, you can better cover this information in class before you give the test.

C. Your testing periods should be set up when you write up your syllabus.

D. Give 3 to 4 tests per nine week period to high school students.
   1. In chemistry, a test may cover one chapter or several chapters.
   2. In math, you usually test after each chapter.
      a. Occasionally, I will test more often.
   3. The younger your students are, the more tests you will want to give them. These tests should probably be shorter, also.

E. Writing a test.
   1. You start at the beginning of the chapter or the information that you are going to go over.
   2. Try to keep in mind the types of questions that you want to ask; multiple-choice, short answer, essay, etc.
   3. As you go through the chapter, start writing down your

questions.
   a. Just list them right down a sheet of paper or on a legal pad or on your word processor.
   b. Do not try to organize them as you go.
   c. Try to write about 25 to 30 questions.
4. Once you have your list of questions, go through them and make any additions or deletions until you have about 25 or 30 questions.
   a. High school science students can handle about this number in a 55 minute period.
   b. If you are short on questions, or you need some alternative questions, take a look at the chapter summary and the chapter review or any old tests that you may have.
5. Label the type and number of each question.
   a. For example: Definition #4.
   b. This helps in grouping the same types of questions together and figuring out the point value for a question.
   c. On the computer, I use the cut and paste to group questions.
6. Assign a point value to each question.
   a. My tests are always worth 100 points. Many teachers do not worry about this. They just assign any value to a question.
   b. Add up your types of questions. For example:

           4 Multiple-choice
          10 Completions
           5 Definitions
           4 Short Answers
           2 Essays
          _____

          25 Questions

   c. On the average, each question will be worth 4 points. You could assign a value of 4, but if you feel essays are worth more, you could assign a value of 3 points each for the multiple-choice and 6 points each for the essay questions. This would give you the following results.

           4 Multiple-choice @ 3 points  =   12 points
          10 Completion @ 4 points       =   40 points
           5 Definitions @ 4 points      =   20 points
           4 Short Answers @ 4 points    =   16 points
           2 Essays @ 6 points           =   12 points
                                             _____
                                             100 points

   d. You may want to add or delete a question, to make

your totals work out.

7. Easy questions should come first in your test.
   a. Every student should be able to answer the first question.
   b. Do not spook a student by placing your hardest questions first.
   c. Put your hardest and most demanding questions at the end of your test. You should have at least one question that will challenge even the brightest students.

8. Your test should be typed. (See sample E)
   a. Use a word processor if you have access to one. They save a lot of time.
   b. Use plain white paper and a black ribbon. This way you will have duplicating masters.
   c. Start with a space for the student's name:
      Name _____
   d. Type the course name, for example, Modern Chemistry.
   e. Type chapter or unit number. This helps you file your tests and your test masters.
   f. Give the total points possible.
   g. Give the directions for the test.
      1. For example: "Please write in the best answer(s) in the space provided." This helps you when you grade their papers. If a student starts to argue about a question, you can tell him he didn't have the best answer.
      2. Students should know what they are expected to do.
   h. Start each group of questions with the point value and the directions.

9. Make sure you give students ample room to write their answers.

10. If you use multiple-choice questions, make sure your correct answers are randomly positioned. If you do not, students will soon figure out that answer #2 is the most common answer.

11. Make sure all words are spelled correctly. Use your computer to check your spelling.

12. Use the best possible grammar and punctuation.

13. On semester tests, I have students put all of their answers on a special answer sheet. This makes grading a lot faster.

F. Run off enough copies for 2 to 3 years.
   1. Keep all tests in a manila folder with the test masters and answer key. You will always know where your masters

and answer key are.
2. Each folder should have the same label as your test.
3. Keep tests filed by the order of your syllabus.

G. Giving a test.
1. Seat students as far from one another as physically possible. This helps prevent cheating.
2. All students should be quiet and should have their desk cleared before the tests are distributed.
3. Make sure students know how long they have for the test.
4. Give out any special instructions.
5. Pass out tests. You should give each student his test individually, so that you can check his desk top and his hands for notes or other aids.
6. Advise students to raise their hand if they do not understand a question or direction.
7. Move around the classroom as they are taking the test. Some teachers do other work as students take their tests, while this saves the teacher time, it may be encouraging a student to cheat.
8. As students turn in their tests, make sure you give them an assignment. This keeps them quiet so they don't disturb the students who are still working on their tests. In my science classes, I may let them read Science Worlds or a library book instead of an assignment.
9. Give slower students plenty of time.
   a. If the bell rings, I let the slower students have a couple of extra minutes.
   b. Dismiss the other students by saying, "As soon as you turn in your test, you are free to go."

H. Grading a test.
1. Flairs make very good grading pens. Use a different color for your answer key. This helps keep you from mistakenly grading your answer key instead of the student's paper.
2. Give partial credit whenever possible.
   a. This encourages students to try. Trying is very important to our society.
   b. It is not necessary to deduct points, but at least bring spelling errors to the student's attention.
   c. Students like written comments about their answers.
4. Total the number wrong for each page, and record the total in the lower left hand corner; i.e. "−5."
5. Try grading every first page first.
   a. This makes your grading more uniform throughout the group of tests.
   b. When grading the second pages, you will probably

not know who the student is. Knowing whose paper it is that you are grading, can effect your decisions.

6. After grading the whole test, add up all the left hand corners and subtract from 100. This will give you their score and percentage. Put this score at the top of the front page.

7. If a student has done well or has shown improvement, I usually add a comment by their score; i.e., Very Good!

I. Handing back tests.
   1. Try to hand back tests the next day, even if it kills you.
      a. Students need the reinforcement and the learning from going over their tests.
      b. Grading old tests can hurt your attitude and drain your energy.
   2. List scores on the blackboard. Students need to know where they stand among their classmates.
   3. Before handing out the tests, this is a good time for a pep talk.
   4. Teacher should hand out the tests. Some students are very sensitive about their grades and do not want other students to see them.
   5. Ask for questions on the first page, then second page, etc.
   6. If you find that you made an error on a paper, do not be afraid to correct your mistake.
   7. If a student thinks he is right and you know he is wrong, have him make a note on his test at the top of the page and tell him you will look at it again when you record their grades. Do not let them argue with you. I also ask some students to come in after class.
   8. Collect tests.
      a. Do not let students keep tests. They will keep test files from your class for future students.
      b. If you have students' tests, you can always show them to a parent. I stack them in a locked cabinet, one group of tests on top of another.
      c. Save old tests for one year and then burn them.
      d. If your old tests are not floating around, you can use them in the future.

J. Record test scores. Use a special color ink for tests in your grade book. Input your scores into the computer as soon as possible.

K. Essay tests are the easiest to make up, but the hardest to grade and the most time consuming.

L. Objective tests are the hardest to make up, but the easiest to grade.

M. Old tests should be re-evaluated every two to three years.

N. Book tests are not a very good way to evaluate your students, however they can serve as a guide to a beginning teacher.

# XVI. Grading

A. Grading is probably one of the hardest jobs that a teacher has to do. Some students just do not fit into a grading system.

B. Before your first day of teaching, make sure you have set up your system of evaluation.
   1. Type up a copy of your grading system, so that you can hand out a copy to your students at the beginning of the semester. (See Sample B)
   2. If this is your first year in a school system, you should have your principal OK your grading scale.

C. Keep your system simple.
   1. This helps your students and parents understand how you determine their grades.
   2. The simpler your system of grading, the easier it will be to determine a student's grade at the end of the quarter. A little foresight, can save you hours of figuring.
   3. A simple system is easier to adapt to a computer grading system.

D. I grade my students on a points system
   1. If the student receives the following point totals, then he will receive the corresponding grade:

   | | | |
   |---|---|---|
   | A | — | 93 - 100 |
   | B | — | 85 - 92 |
   | C | — | 77 - 84 |
   | D | — | 70 - 76 |
   | F | — | Below 70 |

This can be expanded for pluses and minuses. (See Sample B)
   2. Points may be earned in the following ways:

   | | |
   |---|---|
   | Homework | 30 points |
   | Quizzes | 20 points |
   | Use of time in class or lab | 20 points |
   | Tests | 30 points |

   a. If a student does average work on his homework, then he will be given 27 points out of 30. (Since I am dealing with above average students, I feel the average student should receive 90% of the total points possible.) In my grade book, it is easy to find the student's homework average. I simply divide the number of homework grades by 3. For example, let us say that this number is 4. For every 4 +'s, that a student receives then I will add 1 point to 27 or for every 4 —'s I will subtract 1 point. Pluses cancel out minuses. Each zero will subtract 1 point. If a student receives all checks then he will receive 27 points.

   b. To determine a student's quiz points, I add up the points on his quizzes and divide this total by the total number possible, then I multiply this by 20. Sometimes I can save a lot of time by simply giving 4 five point quizzes during the quarter, then I only have to total their quiz scores to get their homework points.

   c. To determine a student's use of time in class or lab, I assign a total of 18 points out of 20 to the average student. If a student does better than average, then he will receive more points. If a student does less than the average then he will receive less points. During the quarter, I will sometimes put a "C−" in my grade book when a student causes problems. This will lower his grade by 1 point. A "C+" will raise his grade by 1 point.

   d. To determine a student's test points, I add up the points on his tests and divide this total by the total number possible, then I multiply this by 30. Sometimes I can save a lot of time by giving 3 one hundred point tests. Then I only have to total their quiz scores and divide by 10.

   e. I now add up their points for these four areas and this gives me their quarter grade. You can use either their point totals or a letter grade.

  3. This system works very easily.

  4. Most people find it fairly objective and fair. They like the weighting of the four areas.

  5. Weightings can be changed for different classes and grade percentages.

E. Currently, I have adapted this system to a computer software grading system called Grade Machine by Misty City Software, 10921 129th Place N.E., Kirkland, WA 98033.

  1. It is a very good grading program and can be ordered for Apple or IBM compatible computers.

  2. Computer grading has not saved me time. It takes a lot of time to input grades. It has saved time at progress report time and at the end of the grading period.

  3. It is easier to keep students up-dated on their grades.

  4. Parents and students are very positive about the computer grades.

  5. Students argue less about their grades. The computer seems more fair.

F. The totals in your grade book can be found easier if your grades are color coded. For example, all test scores are recorded in green ink.

G. All grades should be recorded in ink. Pencil will smudge.

H. You can tear out strips in most grade books so that you can type in student's names. These can be stapled back into your grade book for each class.

I. Make sure you put your name and school in your grade book.

J. Make sure you keep your grade book and data disks in a safe place. Teachers have had them stolen or altered .

K. Grades can also be given according to a curve.
1. The total scores are ranked and the teacher marks off those that will receive A's, B's, C's, etc.
2. Many teachers use this method.
3. The disadvantage of this system lies in the fact that it only tells students and parents how a student ranks in one class. It does not measure how much he has learned.

L. No matter what grade system you use, there will be an observable curve. The system I have explained above operates on a curve. For example, the harder the test, the lower the scores.

M. You should mark in your grade book when a student is absent, tardy, or is a conduct problem.
1. I use an "A" for absent and a "T" for tardy and a "C-" for conduct.

N. You should mark in your grade book which students received progress reports.
1. I put a little dash in front of a student's name. Use a different colored pen for the second quarter.
2. I use a "+" for the third quarter.

# XVII. A FINAL COMMENT

Good teaching is a very special art, but it does take a few tools. This guide was designed to share some of my methods with you. It is my hope that you may gain a few seeds, that you will plant them, and nurture them, and reap a better harvest, and then someday, pass better seeds on.

# APPENDIX — SAMPLE A

## ENRICHED CHEMISTRY SYLLABUS

### Fall 2000

| | | | Test |
|---|---|---|---|
| Chapter 1 | Science of Chemistry 8/26 to 9/30 Candle Investigation | | |
| Chapter 2 | Matter and Its Changes Exp. 2: Density | | Sept. 11, 2000 |
| Chapter 3 | Atomic Structure | | Sept. 20, 2000 |
| Chapter 4 | Arrangement of Electrons 9/24 to 9/28 Exp. 3a: Indentification | | |
| Chapter 5 | The Periodic Law Exp. 5: Solving a Chemical Problem | | Oct. 5, 2000 |
| Chapter 6 | Chemical Bonds Exp. 5: (Special Lab Book) Exp. 12: Covalent Molecules | | Oct. 19, 2000 |
| Chapter 7 | Chemical Composition 10/22 to 11/2 Exp. 6: (Special Lab Book) | | |
| Chapter 8 | Equations and Mass Relationships Exp. 13: Determination of Oxy. in $KC10_3$ | | Nov. 16, 2000 |
| Chapter 9 | Two Important Gases 11/9 to 12/6 Exp. 17: Hydrogen Exp. 17b: Oxygen | | |
| Chapter 10 | The Gas Laws | | Dec. 17, 2000 |
| Semester Test | | | Dec. 20, 2000 |

# Appendix — Sample B

## GRADING SYSTEM
### DeSALES HIGH SCHOOL
**Physical Science, Geometry, and Chemistry**

The following point system will be followed for grading in Mr. Simmons' classes:

| | | | | |
|---|---|---|---|---|
| A | 96 - 100 | C | 79 - 81 |
| A− | 93 - 95 | C− | 77 - 78 |
| B+ | 90 - 92 | D+ | 74 - 76 |
| B | 87 - 89 | D | 72 - 73 |
| B− | 85 - 86 | D− | 70 - 71 |
| C+ | 82 - 84 | F | Below 70 |

Points may be earned in the following ways:

| | Maximum per quarter |
|---|---|
| Homework | 30 |
| Quizzes | 20 |
| Use of time in class or lab | 20 |
| Tests | 30 |
| Total | 100 |

Homework will be marked in the following manner:

    a. plus (10 pts.) - good work
    b. check (9 pts.) - average work
    c. minus (8 pts.) - poor work
    d. zero (5 pts., after 3 missing assignments, 0 pts.)

Unexcused late assignments will be marked down (i.e. from a check to a minus) and will not be counted after one week from the due date. Please retain all of your assignments so you can check your scores with your computer print out of your scores.

Most of your quizzes will be 5 points.

All of your tests will be 100 points each.

To start the quarter you will receive 18 out of 20 for use of time. This grade will move up or down according to your conduct, participation, attendance, tardies, etc.

# Appendix — Sample C

## EXPECTATIONS

### Mr. Simmons' Classes

### A. WORK HARD
1. Do your own work.
2. Turn it in on time.
3. Do your memory work.
4. Do a little every day.
5. Be conscientious.

### B. ASK QUESTIONS
1. If you do not understand, then ask for help.
2. Have the teacher go over the material again, or clarify part of it.

### C. TRY AND TRY AGAIN
1. You will never succeed unless you try.
2. Try to be interested.
3. Be inquisitive.
4. Ask questions.
5. Get involved and jump in.
6. Be happy and smile.

### D. BE RESPECTFUL
1. Do not talk when others are speaking.
2. Raise your hand.
3. Listen to your teacher and classmates.
4. Be understanding.

### E. SEEK HELP
1. Do not get help from your friends on your homework.
2. Mr. Simmons will gladly help you. Come to my office.
3. Help is not getting the right answers, but gaining the understanding of how to solve the problem yourself.

### F. EXPECT JUSTICE
1. Do not expect fairness. Teachers cannot help all students the same. Every student has different needs and the teacher may have to help or spend more time with one student than he does with another.

# Appendix — Sample D

## RULES AND REGULATIONS

### Mr. Simmons' Classes

1. All homework is to be handed in at the beginning of the period. You are responsible for putting your paper on my desk before class starts.
2. You are to conduct yourself in a responsible manner.
3. I want no talking in class, except for when you are answering a question, or asking a question, or when otherwise required.
4. Do not leave your seat without permission.
5. No eating in class.
6. Please keep your hands to yourself.
7. Do not touch any equipment in this room without permission.
8. Nobody is to go into the back of this room without permission.
9. Do not turn on any gas jets without permission.
10. Do not operate the windows.
11. Do not mark on the desks or walls.
12. Do not open any cupboard, cabinet, or closet.
13. No horseplay.
14. Report all accidents or problems to me immediately.
15. In case of fire or a fire alarm, leave the room, turn left, and exit the building.
16. Report all burns, injuries, dangerous or broken equipment to teacher immediately.
17. Keep all hair and clothing away from open flames, all equipment, and all chemicals.
18. Report fires to teacher immediately.
19. Wear aprons and goggles at all times in the lab.
20. Please be careful at all times.
21. If you are in doubt about what to do, read the directions, and/or ask for help.
22. If the teacher should have to leave the room, you are to remain seated and study quietly.

# Appendix — Sample E

## MODERN CHEMISTRY TEST

### Electronic Configuration and Periodic Table

SECTION A True or False (2 pts each). Write true or false in the space provided.

1. A striker is used to light a bunsen burner. _____
2. $Li^{+1}$ is larger in size than Li. _____
3. In a given period, the activity of metallic elements gradually decreases. _____

SECTION B Multiple-Choice (2 pts. each) Circle the number of the best answer.

4. A hydrogen ion is the same as a(n)_____
   1. electron    2. neutron    3. proton
5. The transitional elements are found where on the periodic table?
   1. left side    2. middle    3. right side
6. The non-metals are found where on the period table?
   1. left side    2. middle    3. right side

SECTION C Completion (2 pts. each). Supply the answer.

7. Electrons travel in levels called_____
8. Name two types of electromagnetic radiations.
   1. _____        2. _____
9. Electromagnetic radiation is transferred to matter in units or quanta of energy called _____
10. _____ is the metric unit of volume.
11. _____ is the maximum number of electrons in the S sublevel.
12. There are _____ sublevel(s) in the fourth energy level.
13. About 1869, the Russian chemist _____ devised a useful classification system for the elements.
14. A vertical column is called a(n) _____ on the periodic table.

In questions 15-20, give the electron configuration for the following atoms or ions.

15. Ba        4  _____
16. Na$^{+1}$   11  _____
17. Zn        30  _____
18. Br$^{-1}$   35  _____
19. Fr        87  _____
20. Pu        94  _____

21. The first periodic table was arranged according to increasing _____

22. A horizontal row on the periodic table is called a(n) _____

23. The elements in the last column of the periodic table are called the _____

24. Elements with similar properties have a similar arrangement of _____ electrons.

25. The most reactive non-metals are found in the _____ family.

26. _____ is an alkali metal.

27. Another name for the Calcium family is the _____

28. What are X-rays and how are they formed?
    1.
    2.

29. List the maximum number of electrons that are found in the following energy levels:
    K _____
    L _____
    M _____
    N _____

30. An atom is mainly made up of _____

31. In progressing from left to right in a given row on the periodic table, the atoms gradually _____ in size.

SECTION D Definitions (3 pts. each) Supply the best definition.
31. ion -

32. octet -

33. periodic law -

34. electron affinity -

35. ionization energy -

36. How can an atom give off energy?

37. Discuss the value of the period table. (Include the eight most important pieces of information that it would supply you.)

2 pts. Bonus: Who wrote *The Tale of Two Cities?*

# APPENDIX — SAMPLE F

## CHEMISTRY QUIZ
## MASS RELATIONSHIPS
### Chapter 8

**15 points (Question No. 4 is worth 5 pts.)**
*Please show all of your work.*

(1) 1. What is a mole?

2. Find the gram molecular weight for the following compounds.

(1)     a. CO_____

(1)     b. Cupric Chloride _____

(1)     c. $KCO_3$ _____

(1)     d. $(NH_3)_2SO_4$ _____

(1)     e. Aluminum Nitrate _____

(1)     f. Magnesium Phosphate _____

3. A quantity of zinc reacts with sulfuric acid and produces .1 g. of hydrogen. (a) How many moles of hydrogen are produced? (b) How many moles of zinc are required? (c) How many grams of zinc are required?

                   (1) a. _____

                   (1) b. _____

                   (1) c. _____

4. Suppose 30 g. of iron (II) sulfide are treated with enough HCL so that the iron (II) sulfide completely reacts. How many grams of hydrogen sulfide gas will be given off?

                   (5) Answer _____